The Little Book of CONFIDENCE

By Zack Bush and Laurie Friedman
Illustrated by Vitor Lopes

DEDICATED TO YOU –
OUR WONDERFUL READER

THIS BOOK BELONGS TO:

_____

Copyright © 2022 Publishing Power, LLC
All Rights Reserved
All inquiries about this book can be sent
to the author at info@thelittlebookof.com
Published in the United States by Publishing Power, LLC
ISBN: 979-8-9851749-9-1
For more information, visit our website:
www.BooksByZackAndLaurie.com
Paperback

CONFIDENCE.

That's a big word!
Maybe you've heard it, but you're not sure what it means.

Don't worry. You're not alone. There's a lot to know about being **CONFIDENT.** Ready to learn? Just turn the page!

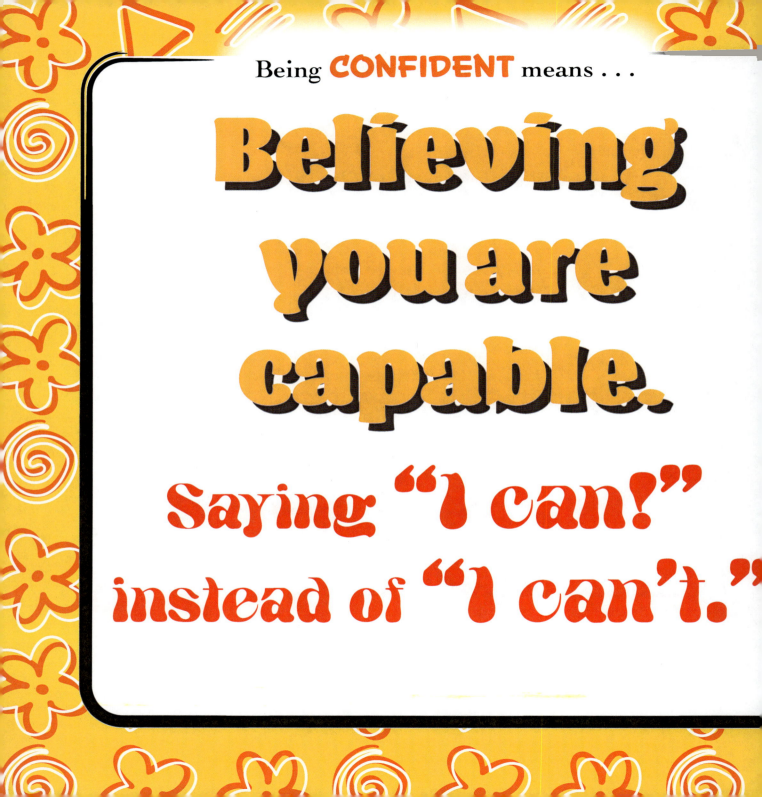

Viewing mistakes as a chance to learn.

Facing challenges, hopeful you will succeed.

Perhaps you're thinking . . .
that sounds good, but how do I become **CONFIDENT?**

Great question!
Here are some tips to help you gain **CONFIDENCE.**

TIP #1:

Always believe in yourself.

TIP #2:
Choose positive words.

Positive self-talk means choosing words to describe yourself that make you feel **CONFIDENT**, then reminding yourself that you are all of those things.

Give it a try! Which words help you feel CONFIDENT?

I am . . .

BRAVE   STRONG

DETERMINED

POSITIVE   KIND

HELPFUL

LOVING

OPEN-MINDED

SMART

SWEET

FRIENDLY

PERSISTENT

You can even develop a mantra, or words you say to yourself every morning, that remind you to stay **CONFIDENT** all day!

TIP #3:

Learn new things.

Learning to do new things
WILL give you **CONFIDENCE**.
You can learn to . . .

Tie your shoes.

Catch a fish.

Swim in the pool.

Play the guitar.

Ride a bike.

Do a cartwheel.

Make your bed.

Set the table.

When you learn how to do something new, be sure to tell yourself, **"Job well done!"**

Then ask yourself how you feel.
Accomplished?
Proud?

You should feel CONFIDENT!

TIP #4:

Set goals for yourself.

Setting goals for yourself and accomplishing those goals will make you feel **CONFIDENT.**

Start small. Be patient. Keep working hard! When you do something you weren't sure you could do, you will feel much more **CONFIDENT.**

TIP #5:

Remember . . . you are not alone.

There are lots of people who believe in you—your parents, brothers and sisters, teachers, and friends.

When you succeed, they will be proud of you, and you will feel **CONFIDENT**.

There are a few more things you should know about what it means to be **CONFIDENT**.

Some days you might be able to do something.

Don't lose your **CONFIDENCE**. Remember your mantra: Get a good night's sleep and know that tomorrow will be another opportunity to try again.

When it comes to feeling **CONFIDENT**, it's important to remember that sometimes you might get tired or feel frustrated or even mad.

But don't give up! Remind yourself you can do it and that making mistakes is how we all learn. Keep working hard and soon you will be doing things you didn't know you could do.

Being **CONFIDENT** is the key to success!

And remember . . . you're not the only person who might not always be feeling **CONFIDENT.**

If you see someone who is having a hard time, be kind and help them out. You might even tell them that the thing they are trying to do is hard for you too.

When you work together, you will help the other person feel more **CONFIDENT**.
And you will feel good as well.

A fun fact: **CONFIDENCE is contagious!**

Still not sure what to do to feel **CONFIDENT?**

Try . . .

Standing up straight.
Wearing your favorite colors.
Thinking positive thoughts.
Sporting a great big smile!

And more than anything . . .

BELIEVE IN YOURSELF!

Feeling **CONFIDENT** takes practice. The more you believe in yourself and your abilities, the more **CONFIDENT** you will become.

Now you know so many ways to feel **CONFIDENT!**

CONGRATULATIONS!
Here's your CONFIDENCE badge.
Go ahead. Print it out. Pin it on.

Go to the website
www.BooksByZackAndLaurie.com
to print out your badge from
the Printables & Activities page.

And if you like this book, please go to
Amazon and leave a kind review.

Keep reading all of the books in
#thelittlebookof series to learn new
things and earn more badges.

Other books in the series include:

The Little Book of Camping
The Little Book of Friendship
The Little Book of Kindness
The Little Book of Presidential Elections
The Little Book of Giving
The Little Book of Government
The Little Book of Valentine's Day
The Little Book of Patience
The Little Book of Father's Day
The Little Book of Kindergarten
The Little Book of Halloween
The Little Book of Grandparents
The Little Book of Laughter
The Little Book of Bedtime
The Little Book of Santa Claus
The Little Book of Good Manners
The Little Book of Pets
The Little Book of Creativity
The Little Book of First Grade
The Little Book of Dinosaurs
The Little Book of the Supreme Court
The Little Book of Sports

Made in United States
North Haven, CT
16 November 2023